Choosing **Scotland's Future**

A National Conversation

Independence and responsibility
in the modern world

August 2007

ISBN 978-0-7559-5493-3

Scottish Executive
St Andrew's House
Edinburgh
EH1 3DG

Produced for the Scottish Executive by RR Donnelley B52638 08/07

Published by the Scottish Executive, August 2007

Further copies are available from
Blackwell's Bookshop
53 South Bridge
Edinburgh
EH1 1YS

The text pages of this document are printed on recycled paper and are 100% recyclable

Contents

Foreword by the First Minister   iv

Summary   vi

1. Scotland's Parliament   1

2. Extending Scottish devolution   7

3. An independent Scotland   18

4. The changing constitution in the British Isles   25

5. Legislation and referendums   31

6. A National Conversation   36

Annex A Reservations in the Scotland Act 1998   41

Annex B Draft Referendum (Scotland) Bill   44

Foreword

The Rt Hon Alex Salmond MSP MP
First Minister of Scotland

We in the Scottish Government are ambitious for the future of Scotland. We also believe that sovereignty in our country lies with its people. As a sovereign people, the people of Scotland – and we alone – have the right to decide how we are governed.

That is why our manifesto for the Scottish Parliamentary elections this year promised to provide an opportunity for the people to consider the concept of Scottish independence in a referendum during this Parliament.

In that election, the people voted clearly for further development of the way we govern ourselves in Scotland. We in the Government believe that independence would be the best for our country. Others support increased devolution, or greater responsibility for taxes and spending, or federalism. But whatever the differences between the political parties, the message of the election was obvious – the constitutional position of Scotland must move forward.

There have also been recent, historic constitutional developments in Northern Ireland and Wales, with new parties coming to government and new responsibilities being devolved. The United Kingdom Government has now published a discussion paper on the governance of Britain.

As First Minister of Scotland, it is my responsibility to explore and lead discussion on the options for constitutional change. I lead the first Scottish National Party Government to be elected in a devolved Scotland, so I will put the case for independence, its benefits and opportunities. However, I also recognise there is a range of other views in our country, and represented in the Parliament.

Scotland's long-standing union with the other nations of the United Kingdom is based on the Union of the Crowns of 1603 and the Acts of Union of 1707 and 1801. The 1801 Union with Ireland has already undergone substantial change. The political debate in Scotland concerns the 1707 political Union, the amendment or repeal of which would still leave the Union of the Crowns intact.

I therefore propose that we have a national conversation on our future to allow the people of Scotland to debate, reflect and then decide on the type of government which best equips us for the future. This paper is intended as the starting point and inspiration for that conversation. It explores areas in which Scotland could take on further responsibilities – such as employment, our national finances, or legislation on public safety such as firearms – as well as the concept of independence, and wider constitutional developments in Britain.

It is now ten years since the referendum to establish the Scottish Parliament. We have seen its potential to respond to the wishes and needs of the people of this country. But we have also seen the limitations of its current responsibilities. I believe it is now time for us, the people of Scotland, to consider and choose our own future in the modern world.

Summary

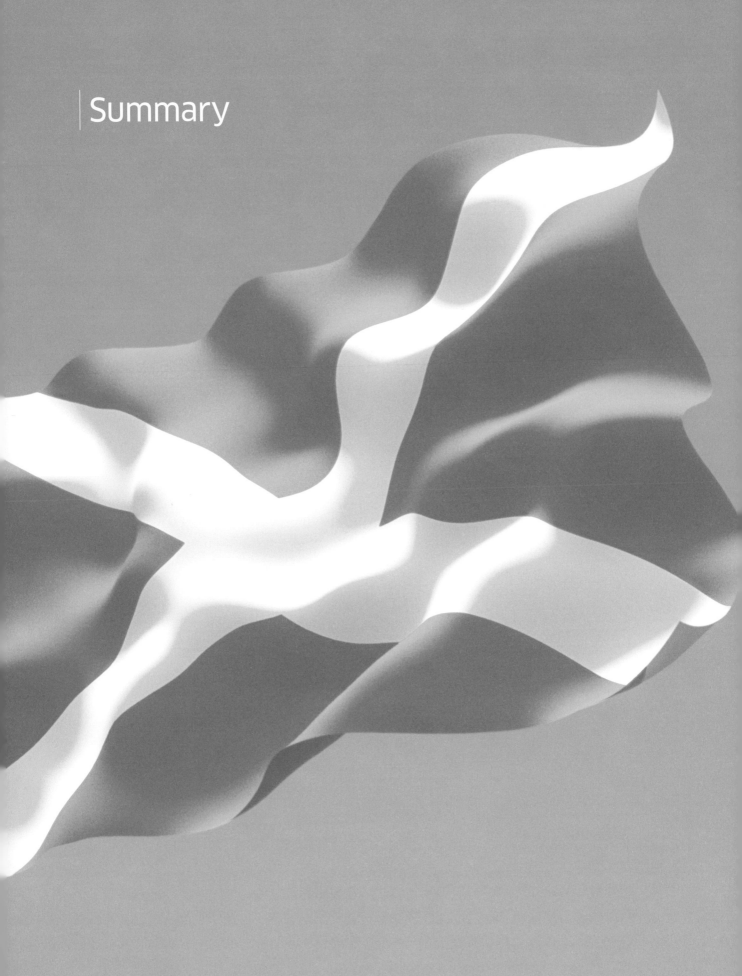

The establishment of the Scottish Parliament under the Scotland Act 1998 gave the people of Scotland a direct democratic voice in decisions across a wide range of government activities already administered in Scotland. The devolution settlement explicitly recognised that the responsibilities given to the Scottish Parliament and Scottish Government in 1999 could be changed, and important mechanisms were included in the Act to allow for further devolution.

Significant powers are currently reserved to the United Kingdom Parliament and the United Kingdom Government. Further devolution in these important areas would allow the Scottish Parliament and Scottish Government to take their own decisions on these issues in the interests of Scotland and reflecting the views of the people of Scotland. In some areas, further devolution could also provide greater coherence in decision-making and democratic accountability for delivery of policy.

To go beyond enhanced devolution to independence would involve bringing to an end the United Kingdom Parliament's powers to legislate for Scotland, and the competence of United Kingdom Ministers to exercise executive powers in respect of Scotland. All of the remaining reservations in the Scotland Act would cease to have effect, and the Scottish Parliament and Scottish Government would acquire responsibility for all domestic and international policy, similar to that of independent states everywhere, subject to the provisions of the European Union Treaties and other inherited treaty obligations.

The nature of the constitution of the United Kingdom is changing. There have been historic developments in Wales and Northern Ireland, and the United Kingdom Government has published proposals to develop further the governance of the United Kingdom. Scotland, whether in the United Kingdom or independent, should continue to play a leading role with our neighbours, taking the opportunity to improve the mechanisms for joint working between governments across the current United Kingdom and with the Republic of Ireland.

Enhanced devolution or independence would require legislation, probably at both Westminster and Holyrood. Substantially enhanced devolution would arguably, and independence would certainly, require the consent of the Scottish people through a referendum. Such a vote, while not constitutionally binding, has been accepted as the correct way of determining Scotland's constitutional future. There must, therefore, be due consideration of appropriate forms of legislation for such a vote, and of the question of how a referendum could be initiated by the Scottish Parliament.

In the Scottish Government's view there are three realistic choices. First, retention of the devolution scheme defined by the Scotland Act 1998, with the possibility of further evolution in powers, extending these individually as occasion arises. Second, redesigning devolution by adopting a specific range of extensions to the current powers of the Scottish Parliament and Scottish Government, possibly involving fiscal autonomy, but short of progress to full independence. Third, which the Scottish Government favours, extending the powers of the Scottish Parliament and Scottish Government to the point of independence. These possibilities are described more fully in this paper.

This paper is the first step in a wide-ranging national conversation about the future of Scotland. This conversation will allow the people of Scotland to consider all the options for the future of the country and make informed decisions. This paper invites the people of Scotland to sign up for the national conversation and to suggest how the conversation should be designed to ensure the greatest possible participation.

1 | Scotland's Parliament

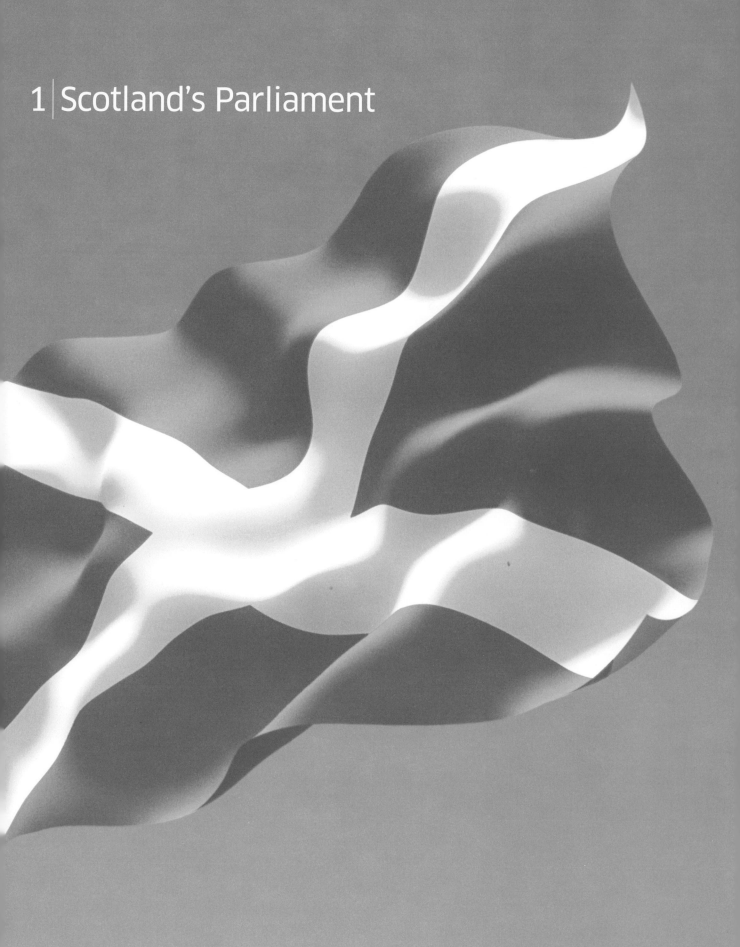

Summary

The establishment of the Scottish Parliament under the Scotland Act 1998 gave the people of Scotland a direct democratic voice in decisions across a wide range of government activities already administered in Scotland. The devolution settlement explicitly recognised that the responsibilities given to the Scottish Parliament and Scottish Government in 1999 could be changed, and important mechanisms were included in the Act to allow for further devolution.

Introduction

1.1 Before the establishment of the Scottish Parliament a large range of government activity was already administered directly in Scotland by the Scottish Office, under separate arrangements from those for the rest of the United Kingdom. However, democratic scrutiny and legislative power still lay at Westminster. The Scottish Parliament now provides direct democratic oversight and has law-making powers across this range of activities. Importantly, the scheme of devolution adopted in the Scotland Act 1998 – where only specified areas are reserved – allows the devolution settlement to evolve naturally as new subjects arise. The devolution arrangements under the Act also contain mechanisms to develop and expand the competence of both the Scottish Parliament and Scottish Government, and the Sewel convention provides the Scottish and United Kingdom Parliaments with a further means to adjust these responsibilities.

Before devolution

1.2 From the establishment of the office of Secretary for Scotland in 1885, through the transfer of the Scottish Office from London to Edinburgh in 1939, to the final form of the Scottish Office before devolution in 1999, the machinery of administrative government in Scotland developed and grew considerably. However, this growth of a distinctive Scottish executive government was not matched by development of democratic oversight, or a legislative body, based in Scotland. Democratic accountability for the Scottish Office was provided at Westminster by Ministers based in London, distant from their departments and electors, to a Parliament similarly remote. Legislation for Scotland, although distinct in its content and application, was taken through Westminster in the same way as other legislation, and was subject to decisions by a majority constituted across the United Kingdom as a whole.

1.3 This situation was widely held to create a "democratic deficit" in Scotland, as the levers of executive government for the country were in the hands of United Kingdom Ministers, sometimes from a party with little electoral support in Scotland. Laws for Scotland were passed at Westminster according to the overall majority of parties within the United Kingdom, without regard to the views of the majority of Members of Parliament for Scottish constituencies.

1.4   The pressures produced by this situation eventually led to the current devolution settlement. Under the Scotland Act 1998, a Scottish Parliament was established to provide direct democratic oversight in Scotland of the range of activities carried out by the old Scottish Office, and to make laws in these areas.

The Scotland Act 1998

1.5   The Scotland Act 1998 devolved to the Scottish Parliament and Scottish Government (known as the Scottish Executive) all matters that are not specifically reserved to the United Kingdom Parliament and the United Kingdom Government. In practice, the areas devolved largely corresponded to those matters that had previously been assigned to the Scottish Office under the responsibility of Scottish Office Ministers (members of the United Kingdom Government), and administered in Scotland by officials from the Scottish Office. The areas devolved included health, education, justice, local government and agriculture and fisheries.

1.6   The reserved areas were areas in which United Kingdom Government Departments had been and remained responsible for services in Scotland, such as social security, health and safety, and tax collection, or areas in which it was considered important to have a common regime across the United Kingdom, such as employment and business law. In addition, the Act reserved matters considered fundamental to the United Kingdom as a state, such as the Head of State and constitution, citizenship, foreign affairs (including representation at the European Union), security and defence.

1.7   Reserved matters are discussed in more detail in the next chapter.

Changing the devolution settlement

1.8   As the Scotland Act devolves all matters not specifically reserved, new subjects that arise – such as climate change – will fall within devolved responsibility, although they may also have features, such as energy, which are reserved. Even without any specific legislative measures to alter devolved or reserved competence, the devolution settlement will, therefore, inevitably develop over time. The United Kingdom and Scottish Governments, and the Westminster and Holyrood Parliaments, must have a dynamic relationship as devolved and reserved responsibilities evolve in response to events and developments.

1.9   The Scotland Act itself also contains important provisions to allow the devolution settlement to be changed legislatively, so executive or legislative competence can be transferred from the United Kingdom Parliament and United Kingdom Government to the Scottish Parliament and Scottish Government. These powers are exercised after consultation between United Kingdom and Scottish Ministers, and consideration and approval at both Holyrood and Westminster. Under section 30(2) of the Act, Schedules 4 and 5 can be amended to give Holyrood legislative competence over areas previously reserved. Under section 63, responsibilities can be transferred from United Kingdom Government Ministers to Scottish Ministers. "Executive devolution" of this kind does not transfer legislative responsibility to the Scottish Parliament. However, Scottish Ministers can still be held to account by Holyrood for the exercise of these powers.

1.10 It is important to note that the Scotland Act itself does not contain any limitation on the use of these provisions to alter the boundaries of devolution. The Act therefore sets up a system of "unlimited" devolution, in which any reserved matters could be devolved to the Scottish Parliament, using the mechanisms already in the Act. No further primary legislation would be required at Westminster or Holyrood.

Westminster and the Sewel convention

1.11 Under the present form of devolution, the United Kingdom Parliament remains sovereign and is able to legislate even in devolved areas (this is explicitly recognised in section 28(7) of the Scotland Act). It therefore retains the general power to make laws for Scotland in all reserved and devolved areas, including altering the competence of the Scottish Parliament and Scottish Government. This may be done either by explicitly amending the Scotland Act or, implicitly, by passing other legislation that is clearly inconsistent with the Scotland Act or a provision in another United Kingdom statute or an Act of the Scottish Parliament. However, under a constitutional convention (known as the Sewel convention), the United Kingdom Government and the United Kingdom Parliament have undertaken not to exercise legislative powers in devolved areas, or to change the legislative competence of the Scottish Parliament or the executive competence of Scottish Ministers, without the agreement of the Scottish Parliament. This mirrors the operation of the provisions in the Scotland Act, ensuring that both Westminster and Holyrood must agree on such changes to the competence before they may take effect.

Changes to devolved responsibilities and competence

1.12 The responsibilities of Scottish Ministers have been changed on numerous occasions under section 63 of the Scotland Act and by the use of the Sewel convention. These changes have come about from combinations of proposals by Scottish Ministers, proposals by the United Kingdom Government, and proposals by outside stakeholders. The reasons for transferring responsibility vary, but tend to recognise either Scottish Ministers' leading policy interest in an area, or the administrative coherence of Scottish Ministers having responsibility for an area that fits with existing devolved responsibility.

Examples include:

- powers to consent to construct, extend or operate electricity generating stations;
- functions relating to food safety and standards;
- regulations on the supply, purchase, possession or use of fireworks;
- functions under the Regulation of Investigatory Powers Act 2000;
- financial assistance in respect of shipping services carrying passengers between the Highlands and Islands and Northern Ireland;
- funding of rail services provided under franchise agreements; and
- functions in relation to fire authority pensions.

1.13 Alterations of the legislative competence of the Parliament have been relatively rare. One example is the extension of Scottish Ministers' and the Scottish Parliament's competence over railways. In 2004 an order was made under section 30(2) of the Scotland Act which allowed the Scottish Parliament to legislate to allocate rail transport functions to Scottish Ministers. Similarly, following agreement by Holyrood under the Sewel convention, the Railways Act 2005 (enacted at Westminster), gave Scottish Ministers responsibility for rail passenger franchises in Scotland and the provision, improvement or development of railway services in Scotland, including the financing of rail infrastructure.

Proposals for further change

1.14 There have been many proposals for other changes to the devolution settlement since its inception. These have ranged from devolving individual subject areas (such as airguns) to changing the underlying nature of the devolution settlement to a federal system, or to full independence. There have also been calls to establish processes to consider wide-ranging change, for example by convening a further constitutional convention.

1.15 At the Scottish Parliamentary election of 2007, each of the major parties made proposals concerning the devolution settlement. In addition to proposing a white paper on independence, the Scottish National Party made specific proposals to extend the devolution settlement by transferring responsibility for the civil service, for North Sea gas and oil, for broadcasting and for firearms. The Scottish Liberal Democrats proposed a new constitutional convention to examine the best way to devolve new responsibilities, including taxation, to Holyrood. They also proposed that competence over the electoral system, the Parliament itself, the civil service, energy, transport and marine policy should be devolved. In addition, the Scottish Liberal Democrats proposed a joint committee of Holyrood and Westminster to work in partnership on regulatory powers, misuse and control of drugs, control of firearms, asylum and immigration, planning of welfare services and aspects of employment law. The Scottish Labour Party emphasised the continued use of the mechanisms in the Scotland Act to make any necessary changes. The Scottish Conservatives declared themselves open to a debate about the powers of the Scottish Parliament to secure accountability for raising revenues, as well as for spending.

1.16 There have also been systematic examinations of further development of the devolution settlement. In 2006, the Steel Commission, under former Presiding Officer Lord Steel of Aikwood, made comprehensive recommendations, notably concerning fiscal policy. These proposals would move the United Kingdom's constitutional structure towards a federal system. The recommendations were put forward as part of a contribution to a proposed second constitutional convention.

1.17 In 2005, the Scottish National Party published *Raising the Standard*, a consultation paper on independence, as part of a contribution to a possible Independence Convention. That paper developed the arguments for an independent Scotland, and was followed by a paper laying out the results of responses to the paper, and a draft Bill for an independence referendum.

2 | Extending Scottish devolution

Summary

Significant powers are currently reserved to the United Kingdom Parliament and the United Kingdom Government. Further devolution in these important areas would allow the Scottish Parliament and Scottish Government to take their own decisions on these issues in the interests of Scotland and reflecting the views of the people of Scotland. In some areas, further devolution could also provide greater coherence in decision-making and democratic accountability for delivery of policy.

Introduction

2.1   The Scotland Act reserves respectively to the United Kingdom Government and to the United Kingdom Parliament a large range of executive and legislative powers. The former can only be exercised by United Kingdom Ministers, even when powers are being exercised for Scotland. The latter are exercised by normal parliamentary procedure on the basis of the votes of the majority of United Kingdom Members of Parliament.

Reserved matters

2.2   Major areas reserved to the United Kingdom are:

- The constitution, including the Crown, the Union and the United Kingdom Parliament and the civil service;
- National security, security and intelligence services, international relations and defence;
- Fiscal, economic and monetary policy, including money, taxes, public expenditure and the Bank of England;
- Immigration and nationality;
- Companies, health and safety, employment rights and industrial relations;
- Oil, gas, coal, nuclear energy and supply of electricity;
- Road, rail, marine and air transport;
- Social security, child support and pension schemes; and
- Broadcasting.

A full list is at Schedule 5 to the Scotland Act, which is summarised at Annex A to this paper.

2.3   Some reserved matters could be regarded as fundamental to the United Kingdom as a state, and therefore difficult to devolve to the Scottish Parliament while Scotland remains within the United Kingdom. These include: foreign affairs and defence; borders and citizenship; the United Kingdom Parliament; the currency and central bank. However, many of these are today affected by international treaties and membership of international organisations, particularly the European Union, showing that responsibility for these matters can be pooled and shared by governments.

2.4 Other reserved areas are not constitutional in nature, but are central to economic and social policy in Scotland: taxation, fiscal and economic policy; trade and industry, including employment; social security and pensions; energy; transport; equal opportunities; broadcasting; and other societal issues such as abortion and misuse of drugs.

2.5 Further devolution to the Scottish Parliament of individual reserved areas would enable the Parliament to come to its own decisions on each, better reflecting any differences in views between Scotland and the rest of the United Kingdom – and within Scotland – on important policy areas. This chapter examines possible further devolution to the Scottish Parliament and Scottish Government, and how additional responsibilities might be used to make practical changes for Scotland in current areas of strategic priority. However, the main outcome of further devolution would be to allow future Scottish Parliaments, of whatever political complexion, to pursue policies and legislation that they considered to be in the best interests of Scotland.

Effectiveness and accountability

2.6 Extending devolved powers could also clarify responsibilities and improve the effectiveness and accountability of government in delivering its policies.

2.7 In some areas, the division of responsibility between the Scottish and United Kingdom Governments is complex, and can lead to difficulties in effective delivery of policy. It can also lead to confusion over accountability for outcomes. For example, climate change, one of the most important issues of the day, involves both devolved and reserved responsibilities across the economy, environment, energy, transport and housing.

2.8 Extending and clarifying the responsibilities of the Scottish Parliament and Scottish Government could therefore increase their effectiveness in achieving results for Scotland. The Scottish Government would have more flexibility, and greater opportunity to pursue policies which require powers across a wide range of governmental functions. The Scottish Parliament could hold the Scottish Government to account for delivering these policies.

2.9 There would remain a need for the Scottish and United Kingdom Governments to work closely together on a wide range of issues, with the other devolved administrations, with other national governments, and with the European Union institutions where appropriate. Joint working in this way would be helped by clear responsibility and accountability for well-defined areas of policy.

A wealthier Scotland

2.10 The Scottish Parliament and Scottish Government have responsibility for many policy areas that affect Scotland's economic performance, such as education, transport, planning and economic development. However, many other responsibilities in the economic field, including macro-economic policy as a whole, are reserved to the United Kingdom. Scotland therefore lacks the full set of tools for building a wealthier Scotland. For example, devolution of responsibility for economic and fiscal policy would allow a Scottish Government to design a business tax environment calculated to encourage investment in Scotland. In exercising these responsibilities the United Kingdom Government must consider the United Kingdom as a whole. For example, from a United Kingdom perspective, regional variations in the tax system could be seen as distortions to economic activity, rather than tools for the pursuit of economic development appropriate to local conditions in Scotland or elsewhere.

2.11 Devolution of taxation and spending responsibilities as a whole – commonly known as "fiscal autonomy" – would allow the Scottish Parliament and Scottish Government to tailor the overall taxation regime to the levels of public expenditure considered appropriate to the needs of Scotland. The Scottish Government would become accountable to the Scottish Parliament and people for the overall level of taxation, rather than for the exercise of the current, very limited tax-varying powers.

2.12 There could be different levels of fiscal autonomy. The more extensive the tax-raising power, and the less significant the contribution of a block grant from the United Kingdom Government, the greater the degree of fiscal autonomy enjoyed by the Scottish Parliament and Scottish Government. Full fiscal autonomy would involve complete responsibility for every form of taxation in Scotland, and, within the United Kingdom, would need to be complemented by a mechanism for Scotland to contribute from its total tax revenues an equitable charge towards the provision of common United Kingdom services.

2.13 The effect of increasing Scotland's responsibility for its own economic and fiscal policies remains a matter of debate. The Scottish National Party estimates[1] indicate that matching the growth rates of other small European nations could mean an additional £19 billion in the economy by 2015, or £4000 per person resident in Scotland. Extended devolution could give the Scottish Parliament and Scottish Government economic tools similar to those available to comparable independent nations in Europe, and provide the opportunity to improve Scotland's economic position in line with these countries.

2.14 Certain matters concerning companies – such as their formation, regulation and insolvency – are currently reserved. Transferring responsibility for these matters would allow the Scottish Parliament and Scottish Government to respond to Scottish concerns, for example in relation to the effects of

---

[1] *Let Scotland Flourish* (Scottish National Party Policy Document, Edinburgh, 2005)

company regulation on the competitiveness of Scottish industry, or on corporate homicide. Companies are also affected by the general regulatory environment, most of which is either reserved or heavily influenced by European Union regulations. Greater Scottish influence in the negotiation, transposition and enforcement of the full range of regulations would allow Scottish circumstances to be better addressed.

2.15 Competition law is another area of reserved powers affecting the economy. The Office of Fair Trading recently opened an office in Scotland to assist with the Scottish dimension to its work, but a transfer to Scotland of responsibility could better reflect market needs and conditions, subject, of course, to European Union law in relation to competition.

2.16 Regulation of the financial services sector is also reserved. This is an important sector for the Scottish economy and one which is increasingly regulated by the European Union. Greater Scottish involvement could similarly allow the Scottish sector to influence the European Union regime and reflect better specific Scottish circumstances.

2.17 Scotland could also assume responsibility for oil and gas reserves in Scotland and Scottish waters, regulating these with a view to maximising economic production of oil and gas and the overall benefit to Scotland. The people of Scotland could be given an effective say on how this money should be used, perhaps following the example of Norway by investing in a fund designed to provide benefits, not only for today, but for decades, and generations, to come.

2.18 However extensive internal devolution may be, it is necessarily the case that the United Kingdom as a single state would have a single currency, whether sterling as at present or, at some future date, the euro. To join the euro, Scotland would therefore remain dependent on a decision of the United Kingdom Government and a referendum across the whole of the United Kingdom, rather than being able to join at a time best suited to Scottish economic circumstances.

A safer Scotland

2.19 Many criminal justice matters are already devolved to the Scottish Parliament and Scottish Government, but those that are reserved include anti-terrorism legislation and legislation on firearms and misuse of drugs. Further devolution in these areas would enable Scotland to adopt anti-terrorism legislation appropriate to meet the threat faced by the country, balancing the rights of individuals with the needs of national security, in a way consistent with Scotland's own criminal justice system. Scotland could continue to play a full role in United Kingdom and wider European efforts for combating terrorism, including sharing intelligence and cooperation between police forces, as in recent events.

2.20 The Scottish Parliament could also be given full responsibly for firearms legislation, which would allow particular Scottish concerns around airguns to be addressed. Similarly, the Scottish Parliament and Scottish Government could take direct responsibility for a particularly Scottish approach to the law on drug abuse, to provide greater protection to Scotland's communities.

2.21 Security and the armed forces are an integral part of any state, and are likely to remain reserved issues as long as Scotland remains within the United Kingdom. These are discussed further in the next chapter.

A fairer Scotland

2.22 Scotland could be given responsibility for employment and trade union law, and health and safety at work. The Scottish Parliament could consider the balance between the rights of workers and the need for modern, flexible conditions of employment, and the proper level of minimum wages for all ages in the workforce. This would be set within an increasing European Union dimension to employment law (such as the Working Time Directive) where Scottish participation in the negotiations and transposition process could better reflect Scottish circumstances. The legal framework on such matters could reflect Scotland's particular economic needs and industrial relations position, rather than be part of a framework designed to cover the United Kingdom as a whole.

2.23 Much of the existing reserved legislation on health and safety in the workplace is implemented through devolved supervisory agencies, like local authorities, and enforced in the Scottish Courts. There could be advantages in also devolving responsibility for regulations on health and safety to integrate these better with other aspects of Scots law. A separate Scottish advisory body for the Health and Safety Executive – Partnership for Health and Safety Scotland – has already been created. The law on corporate homicide could also be a matter for the Scottish Parliament, rather than Westminster, enabling this issue to be handled in a manner consistent with other parts of Scots criminal law.

2.24 Scotland could also have full responsibility for equal opportunities legislation and enforcement agencies, which are almost entirely reserved to the United Kingdom. This would allow Scotland to deal appropriately with those issues which particularly affect Scotland, such as sectarianism. However, the ability to alter the discriminatory provisions of the Act of Settlement of 1701, now incorporated in the Act of Union of 1707, could not be devolved within the current framework.

2.25 Matters concerning consumer protection are currently reserved, so the Scottish Parliament cannot address difficulties experienced by consumers in seeking redress (this includes regulating consumer credit, and addressing problems of over-indebtedness). Any legislative action required must be taken by Westminster. There have already been difficulties over the provision of consumer education, which the Scottish Government cannot currently fund. There is already a Scottish Consumer Council, and the public advisory agency, Consumer Direct, has a separate presence in Scotland. Otherwise, implementation of consumer law is in large part the responsibility of local trading standards officers working in devolved local authorities.

2.26 The Post Office, as well as postal services and their regulation, is a reserved matter. As in other parts of the United Kingdom, communities in Scotland depend heavily on the Post Office network to provide vital lifeline services to older people and other vulnerable members of the community. Devolution of responsibility in this area could allow more flexibility to support and maintain Scotland's Post Office network. The Scottish Parliament and Scottish Government could gauge the priority of supporting the rural and urban Post Office networks against other priorities for government spending, instead of decisions crucial to some of Scotland's communities being made by the United Kingdom Government. The way in which postal services are regulated and cross-subsidised might also affect the operating framework for businesses in remoter rural areas, particularly in the Scottish islands, and could also be considered directly in Scotland.

2.27 There could be a degree of devolution in tax and benefit arrangements for social security. The Scottish Parliament and Scottish Government could assume the responsibility for the rules concerning eligibility for some benefits or tax credits. United Kingdom benefits and tax credits could be supplemented by Scottish schemes to promote particular social objectives, such as additional support for families, the best start for children, help for certain groups to move from inactivity into work, or a Scottish Social Fund to help low income families access low or no-interest loans. Currently recipients of benefits or tax credits can be penalised if they receive additional support, but the Scottish Parliament could be given the power to legislate in such matters. It would then be possible to ensure that schemes to assist people, for example, allowances for studying or for child care, do not simply result in a loss of other benefits or tax credits.

2.28 The Scottish Parliament and Scottish Government could take responsibility for the level of pension for the older population, and the age at which it begins to be paid. Scotland could then, for example, decide to retain the current retirement age, or seek to adjust the balance between the responsibilities of the individual, the state and employers in the provision of state and private pensions.

2.29 For social security to be devolved effectively, Scotland would have to be fully responsible for the financial implications of its decisions in this area. Any devolution of responsibility for elements of social security would best be accompanied by some further devolution of taxation powers (see the discussion of fiscal autonomy above), rather than relying on existing resources to meet additional costs. It would also be important to consider the arrangements for delivering these services, for example, the arrangements under which the United Kingdom Benefits Agency could administer any separate Scottish benefits or pension regime.

A healthier Scotland

2.30 Poor health has been one of Scotland's persistent problems and one that acts against the overall success of the country. Recent evidence has suggested that poor health prevents Scotland from matching the performance of similar countries in Europe. While Scotland has had devolved responsibility for the health service and health promotion, this has been within the context of an overall budget set by the United Kingdom Government. Greater devolution, particularly fiscal autonomy, would allow Scotland greater flexibility on the level of resources to be dedicated to the health service and how these are to be funded.

2.31 Health is also crucially affected by economic circumstances. Further devolution of the economic tools to make Scotland wealthier and fairer could also have an important impact on the nation's health.

2.32 The Scottish Parliament and Scottish Government could also be given responsibility for important public health issues that are currently reserved, including regulation of the major health professions and taxation of tobacco and alcohol.

A greener Scotland

2.33 Scotland is amongst the best placed countries in Europe to develop new renewable and low carbon technologies. Scotland's waters provide some of the best sites for offshore wave, wind and tidal power and for carbon capture and sequestration. The importance of these technologies can only grow as the implications of climate change for energy supply become clear.

2.34 Currently, energy policy is largely reserved to the United Kingdom Government, which has to consider the needs of Britain as a whole in considering its future energy policy, including policy about the location of public sector investment. In light of its potential for renewable power and other clean energy technologies, Scotland is likely to meet its energy needs without nuclear power, and without adding to existing radioactive waste. The United Kingdom Government might well come to a different decision on nuclear policy for the United Kingdom as a whole, with potential consequences for public sector investment in alternative sources of energy, particularly renewables. There is also substantial concern among renewable and other Scottish generators that the pricing policy for access to the grid is discriminating against energy production in Scotland, despite its comparative advantage as a location for a range of new energy technologies. Greater devolution over energy matters would allow the Scottish Parliament and Scottish Government to give priority to the optimal use of Scotland's natural resources in considering future sources of energy, in improving Scotland's efficiency in using energy, and in growing Scotland's green energy sector. Greater devolution could also provide Scotland with the key regulatory and fiscal policy levers necessary to implement an effective and coherent energy policy.

2.35 The Scottish Parliament and Scottish Government could also be given responsibility for policy across the wide range of issues which would allow Scotland to lead Europe in creating a greener society. At the moment, these matters are split between the Scottish and United Kingdom Governments: for example, Scottish Ministers are responsible for landfill, but not for the packaging that creates much of the landfill in this country. Further devolution might allow a coherent approach to these issues and clear responsibility for delivering a cleaner, sustainable Scotland.

2.36 Another area of importance in shaping a greener Scotland is transport, where responsibilities are shared by the European Union, and the Scottish and United Kingdom Governments. Further consideration of the balance of such responsibilities could allow the Scottish Government greater opportunity to shape green policies, for example, in regulating the transfer of potentially hazardous or harmful materials at sea, and in the environmental regulation of other forms of transport.

2.37 The opportunities for greener policies extend equally to the marine environment. Further devolution of responsibility for planning and nature conservation in the marine environment, extending to the waters between 12 and 200 nautical miles from the shore, would make possible a coherent approach to the management of the seas around Scotland. New functions for the marine environment could be aligned with existing responsibilities for fisheries management, as well as any new legislation for devolved areas, such as sustainable management of Scotland's coastline.

2.38 A greater role could also be given to the Scottish Parliament and Scottish Government for promoting individual responsibility in managing the resources of the planet, including consumption, and preserving biodiversity and habitats. The scope of the policies needed for the Scottish Government to secure these objectives would require a wide range of powers and responsibilities.

A smarter Scotland

2.39 Skills for work is a devolved area, but the United Kingdom Government often leads in the design of employment and skills policies. United Kingdom Government employment and benefit-related policies generally address the wider skills needs of the United Kingdom. These might not be suitable if the implications of these policies for Scotland, and the other devolved administrations, have not been fully considered.

2.40 The Scottish Government is developing a strategy for skills to address Scotland's skills issues, some of which are different from those in the rest of the United Kingdom. Further devolution of powers in the area of employment services could provide greater coherence in decision-making and accountability for delivery of policy on employment and skills development.

A stronger Scotland

2.41 Under present arrangements, relations with the European Union are reserved, because they are considered part of foreign affairs. However, many European Union issues relate to domestic policy matters and many of these are devolved to the Scottish Parliament. So, for example, the Scottish Government is responsible for agriculture and fisheries matters in Scotland, but Scottish Ministers are reliant on United Kingdom Ministers to negotiate on their behalf in Europe. Scottish Ministers can attend meetings only with the agreement of United Kingdom Ministers, even when they are of vital importance to Scottish interests, and Scottish Ministers are only rarely called upon to speak at such meetings.

2.42 While Scotland remains within the United Kingdom, United Kingdom Ministers would normally continue to lead in European Union negotiations. In this role, United Kingdom Ministers have to take into account the range of different interests across Britain in the various areas of community activity, and are accountable to the Parliament at Westminster. However, there could be scope for agreement between the Scottish Government and the United Kingdom Government for Scotland to play a greater role in leading negotiations where vital Scottish interests are at stake, and for the United Kingdom Government to agree that the Scottish Government would have a decisive, or greater, say in developing the United Kingdom's negotiating position before and during discussions. This would allow Scottish Ministers the opportunity to play a greater role, although they would not sit as equals with the representatives of other European countries. Similar arrangements could be made for the other devolved administrations as part of a wider reform of United Kingdom representation at the European Union.

2.43 The United Kingdom Government's policies on immigration and citizenship must reflect the situation across Britain, especially in the south east of England and London. In Scotland, there are very different economic, demographic and social issues relevant to population and immigration. Within the United Kingdom, it might be difficult to devolve responsibility for immigration and citizenship to Scotland, but increased powers to attract new migrants could allow the Scottish Government to address Scotland's needs in an appropriate way.

Other matters

2.44 Devolution of broadcasting would give the Scottish Parliament and Scottish Government responsibility for ensuring that the range of Scottish interests was properly represented by national broadcasters, while maintaining the balance of these networks. There could also be opportunities to encourage the production of programming in Scotland, the development of greater coverage of Scottish affairs and appropriate coverage and support of Scotland's cultural life by these national broadcasters.

2.45 The future of the civil service in Scotland is an area that could be devolved to the Scottish Parliament and Scottish Government. Like the Northern Ireland Civil Service, a Scottish Civil Service could be dedicated to government in Scotland, while preserving and reinforcing its independence and impartiality.

2.46 Devolution of elections to the Scottish Parliament would allow the Parliament itself to take full responsibility for the conduct of its own elections. Any actions needed to improve the elections, and remedy defects, could be taken in Scotland, rather than being dependent on the United Kingdom Parliament and Government.

3 | An independent Scotland

Summary

To go beyond enhanced devolution to independence would involve bringing to an end the United Kingdom Parliament's powers to legislate for Scotland, and the competence of United Kingdom Ministers to exercise executive powers in respect of Scotland. All of the remaining reservations in the Scotland Act would cease to have effect, and the Scottish Parliament and Scottish Government would acquire responsibility for all domestic and international policy, similar to that of independent states everywhere, subject to the provisions of the European Union Treaties and other inherited treaty obligations.

Introduction

3.1 The previous chapter has explored further devolved responsibilities that could be given to the Scottish Parliament and Scottish Government. This chapter considers what additional steps would need to be taken for Scotland to move to full independence, like other countries in Europe and beyond. During the 20th century, over 150 new independent states were created, a large proportion through de-colonisation and the break up of the former Communist states in central and eastern Europe. Independence has therefore become a normal constitutional position for countries like Scotland in Europe and world-wide, and the nature and status of independent, sovereign countries are well understood.

Scotland as a nation

3.2 Scotland's long-standing union with the other nations of the United Kingdom is based on the Union of the Crowns of 1603, and the Acts of Union of 1707 and 1801. These provide the political and legal underpinning of the current constitutional position of Scotland, supplemented by subsequent constitutional legislation, such as the Reform Acts, the Representation of the People Acts, the Parliament Acts, the European Communities Act, the Human Rights and Freedom of Information Acts, and the Scotland Act.

3.3 The Union created by these Acts did not remove from the people of Scotland their fundamental political right to determine their own constitutional future. The Republic of Ireland and the countries of the former British Empire chose to move to independence from similar constitutional arrangements. The people of Scotland remain sovereign and have the same right to choose the form of their own government as the peoples of other nations that have secured independence after periods of union with, or in, other states.

3.4 In terms of the fundamental Acts underpinning the Union, the Union of 1801 with Ireland has already undergone substantial revision. The Act of Union of 1707 is the focus of debate for further change or indeed repeal; however, the Union of the Crowns of 1603 would continue even after repeal of the 1707 Act.

3.5   Scotland is a recognised political and territorial entity, with its own legal system, borders, and other independent institutions, some of which were deliberately retained within the Union as conditions of its coming into and remaining in effect. Its territorial extent is not disputed. Scotland's maritime boundaries and share of the continental shelf would need to be formally set down, but there are well-established legal principles for doing so.

3.6   Scotland therefore already possesses certain essential elements of statehood: an agreed territorial extent, and an acknowledged political and institutional identity. The people of Scotland have a continuing right to determine their own constitutional position, whether they choose that of an independent sovereign state, or that of membership of the United Kingdom as at present, with or without enhancement of the devolution scheme.

The Scottish Parliament in an independent Scotland

3.7   For Scotland to achieve full independence, the United Kingdom Parliament must cease to have competence to legislate for Scotland and the United Kingdom Government must cease to have competence in respect of executive action in Scotland. Correspondingly, the Scottish Parliament and Scottish Government would assume the full range of competence, duties and responsibilities accorded to sovereign states under international law.

3.8   Renunciation of the competence of the United Kingdom Parliament to legislate for Scotland would require an Act of that Parliament, which would exclude Scotland from its territorial competence and otherwise recognise the status of Scotland as an independent sovereign state. Consequentially, the composition of the House of Commons would have to be changed to remove representation of Scottish constituencies. Further detailed provisions of that Act and complementary legislation in the Scottish Parliament would reflect the outcome of the negotiations between the Scottish and United Kingdom Governments that would precede the transition to independence.

3.9   Scottish legislation concerning the transfer of competence and achievement of independence would need to re-establish the Scottish Parliament on a foundation other than an Act of the United Kingdom Parliament, that is the Scotland Act. Initially, however, it would not be necessary to change the essentials of the framework laid out in the Scotland Act, and legitimised by broad consensus in the country following on the work of the Scottish Constitutional Convention and the referendum of 1997. Membership, elections, chamber and committee structures and proceedings, standing orders and legislative procedures could all continue in their current form. In other aspects, for example, concerning the judicial review of legislation for conformity with human rights obligations, provisions would have to be made to reflect the new circumstances of independence.

3.10 Similarly, the current provisions for an executive branch laid out in the Scotland Act would also provide an initial model for the government of an independent Scotland. The structure of First (or Prime) Minister, Cabinet and Junior Ministers, and Law Officers, and the framework for their powers and accountability to Parliament, would provide a functioning institutional arrangement, although the underpinning legislation is again likely to require extensive revision.

3.11 The Scottish courts and judiciary would remain constituted as at present, but with cessation of appeals beyond the Scottish courts either to the House of Lords and Privy Council, or (in due course) to the United Kingdom Supreme Court. As noted, provision would need to be made concerning the scope of judicial review both in respect of legislative powers of the Scottish Parliament and in respect of executive powers of Ministers. Arrangements would be needed to secure the continuing independence of the judiciary.

3.12 With independence, the Scottish Government would assume from United Kingdom Government Ministers full Ministerial responsibility and functions for currently reserved areas, in addition to their existing powers in devolved areas, and would be accountable to the Scottish Parliament for their exercise of these responsibilities. Consideration would need to be given to the Ministerial and official structure required to support additional functions, and the appropriate arrangements for Parliament to exercise its scrutiny function. This might involve some expansion or re-organisation of existing capacity within the Scottish Government, as well as the committee structure and other business at Holyrood.

3.13 The future of existing cross-border or United Kingdom public bodies would need to be decided, with a view to ensuring continued effective co-operation, while bringing such bodies, as far as they operate in Scotland, within the competence of the Scottish Parliament and the Scottish Government, so as to provide proper accountability and democratic scrutiny of their actions in Scotland. Consideration would also have to be given to the pay, and other terms and conditions, of employees of continuing cross-border service providers, as well as any current United Kingdom-wide pay agreements.

Negotiations with the United Kingdom Government and others

3.14 Transition to independence would require negotiations between the Scottish and United Kingdom Governments in relation to the terms of independence, as well as the arrangements for the transition itself. These negotiations would have to cover sharing the assets and liabilities of the United Kingdom between the remaining parts of the United Kingdom and an independent Scotland. These would include such matters as: apportionment of the national debt; allocation of reserved assets, such as the United Kingdom official reserves, the BBC, and overseas missions of the Foreign Office; future liabilities on public sector pensions, and social security benefits; the split of the defence estate and the equipment of the armed forces.

3.15 Mechanisms would need to be devised to tackle areas of common interest, such as the succession to the throne (as the Union of the Crowns of 1603 would continue). The position of individuals in reserved areas of public service would need to be agreed, particularly the options for those in the armed forces, the diplomatic service and home civil service, and the Revenue and Customs service. Any issues concerning the borders of an independent Scotland, particularly the continental shelf, would also have to be negotiated, but in a manner that respects the governing principles of international law in such matters.

3.16 These issues are likely to be dealt with in an overall agreement between the United Kingdom Government and the Scottish Government, enshrined in legislation enacted at both Westminster and Holyrood, to allow both Parliaments the opportunity to consider and agree matters affecting both Scotland and the rest of the United Kingdom.

3.17 At the beginning of such a process of negotiation, arrangements should be agreed for arbitration under the principles of international law of any issues which the parties find themselves unable to resolve by mutual agreement.

3.18 Negotiations would also be required concerning the terms of Scotland's (and the rest of the United Kingdom's) continuing membership of the European Union and other international bodies to which Scotland currently belongs as a component nation of the United Kingdom. Such negotiations would necessarily involve both the Scottish and United Kingdom Governments, together with international partners.

Consequences of independence

3.19 The major consequence of independence would be the assumption by the Scottish Parliament and Scottish Government of responsibility for those areas reserved to the United Kingdom Parliament and the United Kingdom Government. The significance of this change would depend on the extent to which further responsibility had previously been devolved to the Scottish Parliament and Scottish Government in the areas discussed in the last chapter. However, an independent Scotland would have responsibility for macro-economics, defence and foreign affairs in a way that would not be possible while Scotland remains within the United Kingdom.

Foreign affairs

3.20 An independent Scotland would be recognised as a state in its own right by the international community. It would be able to develop its own foreign policy to promote Scotland's interests internationally, and engage with other states as an equal partner. It would be able to negotiate memberships of international organisations, or enter or withdraw from such bodies, in the same way as other independent nations.

3.21 An independent Scotland would continue in the European Union and bear the burdens and fulfil the responsibilities of membership. Following negotiations on the detailed terms of membership, Scotland would be in a similar position to other European Union member states of a similar size. As a full member of the European Union, Scotland would have the normal rights of representation in its institutions, with an equal status to the other member states. For example, Scotland would expect representation in the European Parliament nearer to that of Denmark, which has 14 members, rather than the current seven members that represent Scotland (which may be reduced to six). Scotland would be bound by the laws of the European Union, but on a level playing field with other full member states. The distinctive interests of Scotland as a member state would be properly represented through the Council of Ministers and the European Council, and the required transposition of European directives and regulations into domestic law would be done with due regard to their effect in Scotland.

3.22 With independence, Scotland would become a full member of the United Nations and other international bodies, such as the Commonwealth, the World Health Organization, the Organisation for Economic Co-operation and Development and the World Trade Organisation. This would give Scotland its own voice on the international stage, allow the distinctive views of its people to be expressed on the range of issues facing the world today, and allow Scottish Ministers to argue for Scottish interests in international negotiations directly affecting the interests of the nation (for example, on international trade).

Defence

3.23 An independent Scotland could also develop its own voice, and its own distinctive contribution, in the area of defence. Scotland has a proud military tradition, which was represented in the historic Scottish regiments, and the naval, army and air force bases that have for many years provided a home in Scotland for the armed forces of the United Kingdom. With independence, Scotland could decide to continue with membership of current international defence alliances, principally NATO, or could opt, like Ireland and Sweden, for a defence posture outside a nuclear-armed alliance but within other co-operation bodies, such as the Organization for Security and Co-operation in Europe, the Western European Union and the Partnership for Peace programme. An independent Scotland would also have to consider the role and scale of its armed forces, and might choose to emphasise international peacekeeping and disaster relief missions. Independence would allow the people of Scotland, the Scottish Parliament and the Scottish Government to have the final say in all of these matters, and in whether Scottish armed forces participate in military actions, such as Iraq.

3.24 An independent Scotland could accede to the Nuclear Non-Proliferation Treaty as a non-nuclear weapon state, as have other successor states to nuclear weapon states. Scotland could not then possess nuclear weapons. The nuclear-armed submarines of the Royal Navy would have to be removed from Scotland,

and based elsewhere. Whether the remainder of the United Kingdom continued to retain a nuclear deterrent would be a matter for that state to decide.

The countries of Britain as United Kingdoms and European partners

3.25 On independence, Her Majesty The Queen would remain the Head of State in Scotland. The current parliamentary and political Union of Great Britain and Northern Ireland would become a monarchical and social Union – United Kingdoms rather than a United Kingdom – maintaining a relationship first forged in 1603 by the Union of the Crowns.

3.26 Within this relationship, a broad range of cultural, social, and policy initiatives would continue and it is likely that both an independent Scotland and the remainder of the United Kingdom would seek to maintain a series of cross-border partnerships and services. As members of the European Union, both would enjoy full access to each other's markets. An independent Scottish Government could also look to build on the existing close working relationships within the current United Kingdom and with the Republic of Ireland, and could maintain partnership and co-operation through an effective British-Irish Council (further discussion of the British-Irish Council is in the next chapter).

3.27 Independence for Scotland in the 21st century would reflect the reality of existing and growing interdependence: partnership in these Islands and more widely across Europe.

4 | The changing constitution in the British Isles

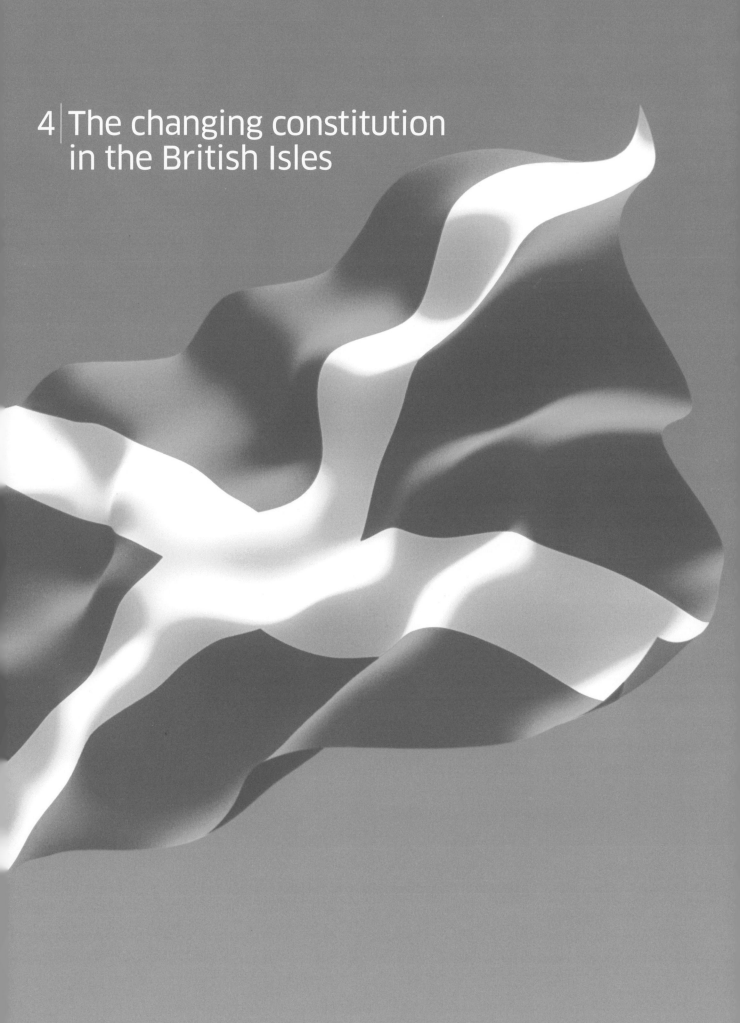

Summary

The nature of the constitution of the United Kingdom is changing. There have been historic developments in Wales and Northern Ireland, and the United Kingdom Government has published proposals to develop further the governance of the United Kingdom. Scotland, whether in the United Kingdom or independent, should continue to play a leading role with our neighbours, taking the opportunity to improve the mechanisms for joint working between governments across the current United Kingdom and with the Republic of Ireland.

Introduction

4.1   Significant changes to the constitution of the United Kingdom were begun in 1997 with the referendums for devolution in Scotland and Wales, followed by reform of the House of Lords, devolution and a directly elected mayor in London, and incorporation of the European Convention on Human Rights into domestic law. Recently there have been further, historic developments in the new Government of Wales Act 2006; the change in administration in the Welsh Assembly Government; and the re-establishment of the devolved assembly in Northern Ireland. The United Kingdom Government has now published a green paper, *The Governance of Britain*, proposing constitutional reform of the United Kingdom as a whole.

4.2   These developments indicate that the process of constitutional change begun in 1997 is continuing. Recent elections in Scotland, Wales and Northern Ireland have demonstrated public support for further consideration of the constitution of the United Kingdom, and the formation of new governments in all three devolved administrations has pointed to the need for formal mechanisms for governments to work together within the United Kingdom and with the Republic of Ireland.

The nature of the United Kingdom today

4.3   The United Kingdom now has three devolved administrations – in Scotland, Northern Ireland and Wales – each with different powers and responsibilities, and each with political parties or coalitions in government different from the United Kingdom Government, and from each other. There is also a directly elected assembly, and mayor, in London, although no other region of England has chosen to have a directly elected assembly.

4.4   The United Kingdom has not developed a traditional devolution or federal model, in which each of the constituent units of the state would have similar powers and responsibilities, with a single coherent set of powers vested in the state's central legislature and executive government. The approach in the United Kingdom, sometimes known as asymmetric devolution (an expression also applied to the Spanish system), recognises the different nature and history of each of the countries. However, it also leads to anomalies between regions and inconsistencies, the best known of which is the West Lothian question, which arises as there is legislative devolution in Scotland (a devolved assembly with the power to pass its own laws), but none specifically for England.

4.5 Developments in Northern Ireland and the new Government of Wales Act 2006, as well as the election result in Scotland, indicate that the trend in the United Kingdom is likely to be for greater devolution from the United Kingdom Government and United Kingdom Parliament to the devolved administrations. However, these developments have not yet been matched by any devolution in, or for, England.

4.6 A further consideration is the development of the European Union, in which sovereign states "pool" elements of their sovereignty for particular purposes, for example a single market. This analysis can also be applied to federal states, where constituent parts of the federation have agreed on the powers of the central government. This analysis has not generally been applied to the institutions of the United Kingdom, that is England, Scotland, Wales and Northern Ireland have not been regarded as pooling their sovereignty, on a continuing basis, to form the United Kingdom Government and Parliament. Instead, the process of decentralising powers and responsibility in the "incorporating union" which created the United Kingdom has been regarded, and described, as devolution. It might be that the concept of pooling sovereignty becomes more applicable as more responsibility is devolved within the United Kingdom, or if the United Kingdom were to develop as a looser association of states (and regions) on the islands of Britain and Ireland.

United Kingdom green paper – *The Governance of Britain*

4.7 On 3 July 2007, the United Kingdom Government published a green paper on the constitution of the United Kingdom, entitled *The Governance of Britain*. The paper has four aims:

- to invigorate democracy, increasing pride in participation at every level;
- to clarify the role of local and central government;
- to rebalance power between government and Parliament, giving the latter more power to hold the government to account; and
- to work with the British people to achieve a stronger sense of what it means to be British and to launch an inclusive debate on the future of the United Kingdom's constitution.

These are covered in four chapters:

- Limiting the power of the executive: this includes proposals to move prerogative powers to Parliament such as deploying troops overseas, ratifying treaties and dissolving Parliament;
- Making the executive more accountable: specifically in the areas of security and intelligence, and statistics and expenditure. This chapter also discusses the roles of the new Ministers for Regions;

- Re-invigorating democracy: this chapter discusses reform of the House of Lords and the House of Commons, direct democracy, and touches on devolution; and

- Britain's future: the citizen and the state, which explores national identity and developing a statement of British values.

4.8 Many of the areas covered in the paper are of direct concern to Scotland: some are in devolved areas, such as the exercise of the prerogative power of mercy; and some are reserved, but affect Scotland directly, such as the future of the civil service and reform of the House of Lords. The national debate on British values is also a proposal of direct concern to Scotland, although in Scotland this debate will also concern the values that contribute to a resurgent Scottish identity, as well as the British values which will be prominent elsewhere in the United Kingdom.

4.9 Other areas covered in the paper are mainly of concern to England and Wales, but have parallels in Scotland. These include the role of the Attorney General, the appointment of the judiciary, and the re-invigoration of local and national democracy. In many of these areas, Scotland has already moved forward from the position in England and Wales, and there might be valuable lessons that can be learnt by the United Kingdom Government from Scottish practice, for example in the handling of petitions in the Scottish Parliament, or the gathering of evidence from interested parties by Scottish Parliamentary Committees during the progress of Bills.

4.10 There are also proposals on the administration of the business of the United Kingdom Government, such as consultation on the Queen's Speech and annual parliamentary debates on the objectives of United Kingdom Government Departments. These could both provide useful models for Scottish Government practice and provide a mechanism for the Scottish Government to contribute to the United Kingdom Government's policy formulation in non-devolved areas which impact on Scotland.

4.11 The green paper does not discuss, from a United Kingdom point of view, the issues raised in this paper: further development of devolution to Scotland, or to other parts of the United Kingdom (for example, there is no discussion of the West Lothian question). The paper reasserts the current constitutional arrangements for the United Kingdom, and that the United Kingdom Parliament remains sovereign.

4.12 The Scottish Government will provide a detailed response to the United Kingdom Government on its proposals in due course. It will also be necessary to consider with the United Kingdom Government how to co-ordinate with, and contribute to, the national discussion it proposes to have on its green paper.

Joint Ministerial Committees

4.13 The results of elections across the devolved administrations this year have highlighted the need for sound formal mechanisms for the governments of the United Kingdom to work together. The arrangements for liaison were set out on devolution in the Memorandum of Understanding, at the apex of which sits the Joint Ministerial Committee. The Joint Ministerial Committee was intended to provide a forum for United Kingdom Ministers and devolved Ministers to discuss matters of mutual concern. The framework provides for a plenary format and a range of sub-committees.

4.14 In future the Joint Ministerial Committee could provide a vehicle for the co-ordination of policy work and formal consultation between Ministers and officials, complementing other contacts. The Scottish Government would propose to work with the United Kingdom Government and the other devolved administrations to place the Joint Ministerial Committee on a sound footing. This could include re-establishing the plenary format of the Joint Ministerial Committee, and considering the scope for a range of sub-committees to conduct more detailed work. The Joint Ministerial Committee could also ensure that the Memorandum of Understanding and bi-lateral concordats provide a sound framework for joint working within the United Kingdom.

British-Irish Council

4.15 There is scope for close working with the Republic of Ireland as well as within the United Kingdom. The British-Irish Council, as established in 1998 under the auspices of the Good Friday Agreement, already provides a forum for joint working across a range of areas, which currently includes transport, environment, demography, e-health, knowledge economy, tourism, social inclusion, misuse of drugs, and minority and lesser used languages. Scotland currently leads the demography work and jointly leads with Wales in the social inclusion strand, and has asked to lead a further sub-group on energy transmission. The supporting secretariat for the Council has recently been tasked to review and renew the work of the Council, and should report at a future summit meeting in late 2007 or early 2008. This may involve an expanded or revised work programme for the mutual benefit of member administrations.

4.16 The Scottish Government proposes to work with all members – the United Kingdom Government, the devolved administrations, the crown dependencies of the Isle of Man, Guernsey and Jersey and the Government of the Republic of Ireland – to ensure that the British-Irish Council is developed as a suitable forum for co-operation across the administrations of Britain and Ireland. An early opportunity for the Scottish Government to progress such development will come when it hosts a future British-Irish Council Summit during 2008.

4.17   The current arrangements bring together two sovereign states, three devolved nations and three crown dependencies to co-operate on issues of mutual concern. This could provide a model for future co-operation across Britain and Ireland following independence for Scotland, bringing together three sovereign states, including an independent Scotland, and the remainder of the United Kingdom, the devolved nations and island territories. This would provide a formal mechanism for the governments of Britain and Ireland to work together to complement other continuing relations across the islands in social and cultural fields, as well as a continuing Union of the Crowns.

5 | Legislation and referendums

Summary

Enhanced devolution or independence would require legislation, probably at both Westminster and Holyrood. Substantially enhanced devolution would arguably, and independence would certainly, require the consent of the Scottish people through a referendum. Such a vote, while not constitutionally binding, has been accepted as the correct way of determining Scotland's constitutional future. There must, therefore, be due consideration of appropriate forms of legislation for such a vote, and of the question of how a referendum could be initiated by the Scottish Parliament.

Introduction

5.1   Further devolution or full independence for Scotland would require further legislation, either under the existing provisions of the Scotland Act, or by new Acts of the Scottish and United Kingdom Parliaments. The particular legislative route chosen would depend on the option to be pursued. The agreement of the Scottish people would be needed for independence, and a referendum would be required to allow the people to express their view, followed by United Kingdom and Scottish legislation.

Legislative options for further devolution

5.2   As discussed above, the Scotland Act already contains mechanisms which can be used to give further legislative competence to the Scottish Parliament. This can also be achieved through United Kingdom legislation, with the agreement of the Scottish Parliament under the Sewel convention. The major point to note is that the agreement of both the Scottish and United Kingdom Parliaments would be required whatever procedure is followed.

5.3   It is for consideration whether any of the options for enhanced devolution, or a combination of them, would require, or would benefit from, the further consent of the Scottish people by way of referendum. The referendum in 1997 was for the principle of devolution, following proposals in a white paper. The Scotland Act (as discussed above) contains provisions for devolution to be extended without further primary legislation, and makes no mention of the need for a referendum. On the other hand, the referendum in 1997 did contain a second question on tax-varying powers, which suggests that certain powers are significant enough to require the specific consent of the Scottish people. However, the vote on tax-varying powers was again on a general principle, rather than a specific proposal. The Government of Wales Act 2006 also allows for a further referendum to confirm the extension of the competence devolved to the Welsh Assembly, but that is against a very different constitutional arrangement as regards the legislative competence of that Assembly.

5.4   Even if no single measure of further devolution would require a referendum, a wide-ranging review of the devolution settlement could be subject to a referendum. A decision on whether a referendum was required for enhanced devolution would need to take into account the range and nature of the proposals, and the view of the public, and could only be taken as these emerged.

Legislative options for independence

5.5   Independence for Scotland would involve a fundamental change in the country's constitutional status, with implications for partner countries in the present United Kingdom. It is generally accepted that the full consent of the people of Scotland would be required by way of a referendum.

5.6   The timing and question of the referendum would need to be considered, as would the legislative basis. There are several possible questions that could be asked in a referendum on independence, for example, agreement to the principle of independence, agreement to negotiate, or agreement to a concluded Act or Treaty with the United Kingdom Government. Some of these could only be asked at a particular time: agreement to negotiate would need to be sought before any negotiations; agreement to a Treaty or Act of Independence could only take place after the terms of the Treaty had been negotiated or the Act had been passed.

5.7   The devolution referendum provides a useful comparison for other referendums, including one on independence. That referendum gave the people of Scotland the opportunity to vote on the principle of devolution based on the proposals set out in a white paper, before the detail of the Scotland Act was established. It provided a clear mandate for the Labour Government to proceed with the Scotland Act 1998 and the establishment of the Scottish Parliament.

5.8   It would be possible to design a referendum with more than one option, to give Scottish electors the choice between independence, the status quo, and significant additional devolution. However, there is not a sufficiently well developed proposal for further devolution to make such a multi-option referendum a realistic proposal at this stage. The design of such a referendum would also raise technical issues on how support for each option is to be judged – for example, whether there would be ranking of options. Despite these considerations, proposals for a multi-option referendum might well be developed into a feasible option during the national conversation.

5.9   As far as legislative competence is concerned, a referendum could be held under the authority of an Act of the Scottish Parliament, depending on the precise proposition in the referendum Bill, or any adjustments made to the competence of the Parliament before the Bill is introduced. Legislation for a referendum could also be passed by the United Kingdom Parliament, most likely consulting the Scottish Parliament for its views. The Act could make detailed provision for the holding of a referendum, setting out the question and other arrangements, or could give Scottish or United Kingdom Ministers powers to bring forward secondary legislation with these details at a later date. A further possibility would be to set up a mechanism similar to that in the Government of Wales Act 2006 that would empower the Scottish Parliament and Scottish Government (or the Parliament alone) to call for a referendum at a time of its choosing, rather than relying on Scottish or United Kingdom Ministers to bring forward proposals. An illustrative draft Bill is described in the text box, and attached at Annex B.

5.10   Unless legislation makes different provision, a referendum proposition is normally taken as agreed to if it receives a simple majority of votes, that is 50% plus one. Some referendums set a higher threshold, for example by requiring a higher percentage of votes in favour or (as in the Scottish devolution referendum in 1979) by requiring a certain percentage of those entitled to vote. While the issues raised by a referendum on independence could be seen as more significant than previous referendums, the purpose of the referendum is to allow the Scottish people to express their view. A higher threshold could obscure the clarity of the outcome and could be seen as an arbitrary device to frustrate their will, like the threshold adopted in the 1979 devolution referendum.

5.11   It has been suggested that there might be two referendums: on the principle of independence, to give the Scottish Government authority to negotiate; and following Acts of Independence being passed by the Scottish and United Kingdom Parliaments. A second referendum would recognise the significance of the decision for Scotland to become independent and allow the people of Scotland the final say on the matter. On the other hand, there are strong arguments against such an approach. One referendum on the principle of independence could give the Scottish Parliament and Scottish Government sufficient clarity and confidence that the people wish Scotland to become an independent state. The prospect of a further referendum could reduce the certainty of the choice facing the people at the referendum, and reduce the impact of the decision that the people make. As a democratically representative legislature, the Scottish Parliament could carry forward the people's will to conclude the arrangements to deliver independence.

Draft Bill for a referendum

1. The form and content of a referendum would depend on the proposition to be put to the people of Scotland, and would in itself be a matter for debate. At Annex B is a draft Bill to illustrate the form that the legislation would take for a referendum held to establish whether the Scottish people agree to authorise the Scottish Government to negotiate terms for Scottish independence with the Government of the United Kingdom.

2. The proposition in the draft Bill is:

    The Scottish Government should negotiate a settlement with the Government of the United Kingdom so that Scotland becomes an independent state.

    This proposition is intended to make clear that the new settlement is not simply about transferring further powers to the Scottish Parliament and the Scottish Government, but would involve full independence for Scotland. This is intended to provide a clear view from the Scottish people on the principle of independence as well as an explicit mandate to negotiate. The draft Bill assumes that a simple majority would be required.

3. The competence of the Scottish Parliament to legislate for a referendum would depend on the precise proposition in the referendum Bill, or any adjustments made to the competence of the Parliament before the Bill is introduced. At present the constitution is reserved, but it is arguable that the scope of this reservation does not include the competence of the Scottish Government to embark on **negotiations** for independence with the United Kingdom Government. Legislative action at both Holyrood and Westminster would be required to effect independence for Scotland or to transfer substantive responsibility for reserved matters.

4. The draft Bill also contains provisions on, or powers to set:

    *   the timing of the referendum;
    *   who is entitled to vote; and
    *   the detailed rules for the conduct of the referendum, from the start of the campaign to the vote and the declaration of the result.

5. In the Scottish devolution referendum in 1997 entitlement to vote was based on residence in Scotland, which is the same as for local government elections. The draft Bill follows this model and does not attempt to define categories of people resident outside Scotland eligible to vote in the referendum, nor to exclude any people resident in Scotland from the poll. The draft Bill envisages an independent Scotland based on the territorial and political entity of Scotland, not on place of birth, or ethnic group.

6 | A National Conversation

Summary

This paper is the first step in a wide-ranging national conversation about the future of Scotland. This conversation will allow the people of Scotland to consider all the options for the future of the country and make informed decisions. This paper invites the people of Scotland to sign up for the national conversation and to suggest how the conversation should be designed to ensure the greatest possible participation.

Introduction

6.1 The current Scottish Government believes that the best future for Scotland is as an independent, sovereign country like so many other European countries. However, this is a decision that only the Scottish people can make for themselves, in the light of all the arguments put forward for independence and by comparison with other forms of constitutional change. The Scottish Government is therefore committed to a national conversation about Scotland's future, which will allow all the options for developing the governance of the country to be fully discussed by the people of Scotland.

The need for a national conversation

6.2 It is now ten years since the referendum on devolution, and eight years since the Scottish Parliament was established. As discussed in this paper, there have been significant recent constitutional developments in Wales and Northern Ireland, and the United Kingdom Government has recently made its own proposals for change. Most importantly, the majority of Members of the Scottish Parliament elected at the Scottish Parliamentary elections this year stood on manifestoes advocating further devolution of responsibilities to Scotland. Events since those elections have illustrated the limitations of the current constitutional settlement, for example the conduct of the elections themselves.

6.3 Eight years of experience of operating a devolved administration for Scotland has given the Scottish Parliament and Scottish Government considerable experience of their responsibilities, and the limitations of the current arrangements. Some extensions have been made to devolved competence, but most of these have been relatively minor in scope. There are therefore good reasons to review now the constitutional settlement embodied in the Scotland Act.

6.4 However, there is no consensus on the next steps that should be taken to develop Scotland's constitutional position, and the parties elected to the Scottish Parliament made a range of proposals. It is also clear that the support of the people of Scotland is necessary to make changes for the future. Hence the Scottish Government proposes a national conversation to allow the people of Scotland to explore and understand their options and to decide their own future.

The scope of the national conversation

6.5   The Scottish Government envisages a national conversation which will consider the entire range of possible changes to the current constitutional settlement for Scotland. The national conversation will allow an informed choice about independence, or other forms of constitutional change. The Scottish Government would intend to make the case for independence, and seek support for a referendum, but also to put to the Scottish people the arguments for other forms of further constitutional change through a programme of events in which the benefits of the options can be fully tested. Other political parties, groups and individuals with different views would also play a full part in the conversation.

6.6   At the end of the conversation, the Scottish Government foresees a choice facing Scotland of:

- continuing with the current constitutional settlement with no or minimal change;
- extending devolved responsibilities to Scotland in areas identified during the national conversation; or
- taking the steps to allow Scotland to become a fully independent country.

An invitation to sign up for the national conversation

6.7   The significance of the questions raised in this national conversation requires the fullest participation possible, and the Scottish Government intends that as many people in Scotland as possible should take part.

6.8   As a first step, the Scottish Government invites people to sign up for the national conversation. The Scottish Government is seeking commitments from groups, organisations and individuals to participate in the national conversation, and an indication of the contributions people would like to make to the debate. The Scottish Government would also welcome expressions of interest from those that want to follow and keep in touch with the debate. Those committing or expressing an interest will be informed of significant developments in the national conversation.

6.9   Given the importance of this conversation, and the importance of full engagement, the Scottish Government would also welcome views on how to design the questions, processes, materials and arguments within the conversation to ensure the greatest possible participation. Possibilities include:

- public meetings and events around Scotland, with the First Minister and other Scottish Ministers, to hear and exchange views with the public;
- events involving other political and civic leaders, business people and public servants, academics and teachers;
- events targeted at local communities, young people, and minority groups;

- public workshops, roadshows, exhibitions and local conferences;

- web-based information and interactive facilities;

- opportunities to contribute in writing and electronically;

- opinion surveys, focus groups and other research methods, such as citizens' panels; and

- support to organisations (including outreach organisations), communities and individuals who want to host their own national conversation events.

6.10 The Scottish Government invites views on these possibilities, and suggestions for any other methods of participation.

How to participate in the national conversation

6.11 The best way to sign up for the national conversation, or to make suggestions for participation events or methods, is to visit the national conversation website at **www.anationalconversation.com** or e-mail joinin@anationalconversation.com.

6.12 Responses can also be sent by post to:

A National Conversation
Constitution Unit
G-A North
Victoria Quay
Edinburgh
EH6 6QQ

Annexes

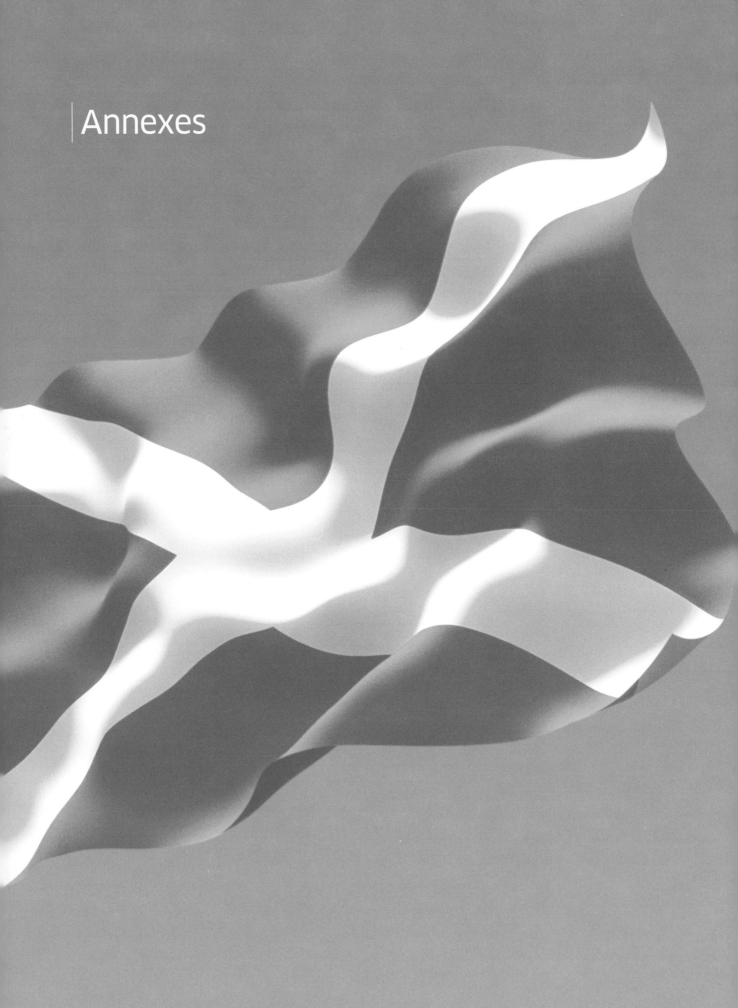

Annex A: Reservations in the Scotland Act 1998

Constitutional and general reservations

- The Crown, including succession to the Crown and a regency
- The Union of the Kingdoms of Scotland and England
- The Parliament of the United Kingdom, elections for membership of the House of Commons, the European Parliament and the Scottish Parliament
- The higher courts
- The Security Service, the Secret Intelligence Service and the Government Communications Headquarters
- The registration and funding of political parties
- Foreign affairs, international relations, and representation
- The civil service
- Defence
- Treason

Economic and fiscal

- Fiscal, economic and monetary policy, including the issue and circulation of money, taxes and excise duties, government borrowing and lending, control over United Kingdom public expenditure, the exchange rate and the Bank of England
- The currency: coinage, legal tender and bank notes
- Financial services
- Financial markets, including listing and public offers of securities and investments, transfer of securities and insider dealing

Home affairs

- Misuse of drugs
- Data protection
- Firearms
- Classification of films and videos
- Immigration and nationality, including asylum and issue of travel documents
- Scientific procedures on live animals
- National security, interception of communications, official secrets and terrorism
- Betting, gaming and lotteries
- Emergency powers
- Extradition

Trade and industry

- The creation, operation, regulation and dissolution of types of business association
- Insolvency in relation to business associations
- Regulation of anti-competitive practices and agreements; abuse of dominant position monopolies and mergers
- Intellectual property
- Import and export control
- Regulation of sea fishing outside the Scottish zone (except in relation to Scottish fishing boats)
- Consumer protection
- Product standards, safety and liability
- Weights and measures
- Telecommunications and wireless telegraphy, including internet services
- Post Office, posts and postal services
- Research Councils
- Designation of assisted areas
- Protection of trading and economic interests

Energy

- Generation, transmission, distribution and supply of electricity
- Oil and gas, including the ownership of, exploration for and exploitation of deposits of oil and natural gas, offshore installations and pipelines
- Coal, including its ownership and exploitation, deep and opencast coal mining and coal mining subsidence
- Nuclear energy and nuclear installations, including nuclear safety, security and safeguards, and liability for nuclear occurrences

Transport

- Road transport
- Rail transport, provision and regulation of railway services
- Marine transport, including navigational rights and freedoms
- Air transport
- Transport of radioactive material

Social security

- Social security schemes
- Child support
- The regulation of occupational pension schemes and personal pension schemes, including the obligations of the trustees or managers of such schemes

Regulation of the professions

- Architects, health professions, auditors

Employment

- Employment rights and duties and industrial relations
- Health and safety
- Job search and support

Health and medicines

- Regulation of medical professions
- Abortion
- Xenotransplantation
- Embryology, surrogacy and genetics
- Medicines, medical supplies and poisons

Media and culture

- Broadcasting, including the BBC
- Public lending right
- Government Indemnity Scheme for objects on loan to museums, art galleries, etc
- Property accepted in satisfaction of tax

Miscellaneous

- Judicial remuneration
- Equal opportunities
- Control of nuclear, biological and chemical weapons and other weapons of mass destruction
- Ordnance survey
- Timescales, time zones and the subject-matter of the Summer Time Act 1972
- The calendar, units of time, the date of Easter
- Outer space

Annex B

DRAFT

Referendum (Scotland) Bill

An Act of the Scottish Parliament to make provision for the holding of a referendum in Scotland on the proposal to negotiate with the Government of the United Kingdom to achieve independence for Scotland.

1   Referendum on independence negotiations

(1)   On (*insert date*), a referendum is to be held in Scotland on whether the Scottish Government should negotiate with the Government of the United Kingdom to achieve independence for Scotland.

(2)   The propositions to be voted on in the referendum and the front of the ballot paper to be used for that purpose are to be in the form set out in schedule 1.

(3)   Those entitled to vote in the referendum are the persons who, on the date of the referendum, would be entitled to vote as electors at a local government election in any electoral area in Scotland.

(4)   But an alteration in a register of electors under section 13A(2) (alteration of registers) or 57 (registration appeals) of the Representation of the People Act 1983 (c. 2) does not have effect for the purposes of the referendum unless it is made before the start of the period of 11 days ending with the date of the referendum.

(5)   The Scottish Ministers must appoint a Chief Counting Officer.

(6)   The Chief Counting Officer must appoint a counting officer for each local government area.

(7)   Each counting officer must—

(a)   conduct the counting of votes cast in the area for which the officer is appointed in accordance with paragraph 9 of schedule 2 and any directions given by the Chief Counting Officer, and

(b)   certify the number of ballot papers counted by the officer and the number of votes cast for each proposition.

(8)   The Chief Counting Officer must certify—

(a)   the total number of ballot papers counted, and

(b)   the total number of votes cast for each proposition,

for the whole of Scotland.

(9)   Schedule 2 makes further provision about the referendum and its conduct.

2   **Legal proceedings**

No court may entertain any proceedings for questioning the number of ballot papers counted or votes cast as certified by the Chief Counting Officer or by a counting officer appointed in accordance with section 1(6).

3   **Short title**

The short title of this Act is the Referendum (Scotland) Act.

SCHEDULE 1
(introduced by section 1(2))

FORM OF BALLOT PAPER

The Scottish Parliament has decided to consult people in Scotland on the Scottish Government's proposal to negotiate with the Government of the United Kingdom to achieve independence for Scotland:

Put a cross (X) in the appropriate box

I AGREE that the Scottish Government should negotiate a settlement with the Government of the United Kingdom so that Scotland becomes an independent state.	

OR

I DO NOT AGREE that the Scottish Government should negotiate a settlement with the Government of the United Kingdom so that Scotland becomes an independent state.	

SCHEDULE 2
(introduced by section 1(9))

CONDUCT OF THE REFERENDUM ETC.

1   The provisions of this schedule have effect in relation to the referendum under section 1.

Time

2 (1)   In calculating any period of time for the purposes of any provision of, or applied by or under, this Act, the following days are to be disregarded.

   (2)   The days are—

      (a) a Saturday or Sunday, and

      (b) a day which is a bank holiday under the Banking and Financial Dealings Act 1971 (c. 80) in Scotland.

Advertisements

3   The Town and Country Planning (Control of Advertisements) (Scotland) Regulations 1984 (S.I. 1984/467) have effect in relation to the display on any site of an advertisement relating specifically to the referendum as they have effect in relation to the display of an advertisement relating specifically to an election for the Parliament of the United Kingdom.

Premises used for referendum purposes

4   In relation to premises, section 98 (premises not affected for rates) of the Representation of the People Act 1983 (c. 2) has effect as if the reference to public meetings in furtherance of a person's candidature at an election included a reference to public meetings promoting a particular result in the referendum.

Returning officers and counting officers

5 (1)   Functions conferred by or under this schedule on the returning officer are to be exercised in each local government area by the person who, under section 41 (local government elections in Scotland) of the Representation of the People Act 1983 (c. 2) is, or may discharge the functions of, the returning officer at an election of councillors for that area.

  (2)   A returning officer may, in writing, appoint one or more persons to discharge all or any of the returning officer's functions.

  (3)   It is the returning officer's general duty at a referendum to do all such acts and things as may be necessary for effectually conducting the referendum in the manner provided by or under this schedule.

6   The council for a local government area must place the services of its officers at the disposal of any person who is acting as returning officer or counting officer in relation to that area.

7   A counting officer may, in writing, appoint one or more persons to discharge all or any of the counting officer's functions.

Hours of polling

8   The hours of polling are between 7 a.m. and 10 p.m.

Counting of votes etc

9 (1)   A counting officer must, in accordance with any directions given by the Chief Counting Officer, appoint persons to observe the counting of the votes and the verification of the ballot paper accounts.

  (2)   No person may attend the counting of votes for any local government area unless the person is—

        (a) a counting officer for that area or a person appointed by such a counting officer by virtue of this schedule,

        (b) the Chief Counting Officer,

        (c) the member of the Scottish Parliament for a constituency wholly or partly within that area,

        (d) a member of the Scottish Parliament for a region which that area is wholly or partly within,

        (e) the member of the Parliament of the United Kingdom for a constituency wholly or partly within that area,

        (f) an observer appointed by the counting officer for that area under sub-paragraph (1), or

(g) permitted by the counting officer for that area to attend the count.

(3) A counting officer must give observers such reasonable facilities for observing the proceedings, and all such information with respect to them, as the officer can give them consistently with the orderly conduct of the proceedings and the discharge of the counting officer's duties in connection with them.

(4) Before a counting officer makes a certification under section 1(7)(b) or makes any public announcement as to the result of the count, the officer shall consult the Chief Counting Officer who may direct the officer to recount the ballot papers.

10 A counting officer must, as soon as possible after the Chief Counting Officer has made the certification required by section 1(8), forward to the Scottish Ministers—

(a) the packets of ballot papers in the counting officer's possession, and

(b) such other documents and information as may be required by virtue of an order under paragraph 11(1),

endorsing on each packet a description of its contents and the name of the area for which the counting officer was appointed.

11 (1) The Scottish Ministers may by order made by statutory instrument make further provision about the referendum.

(2) An order under sub-paragraph (1) may, in particular—

(a) apply (with or without modifications) any enactment,

(b) make provision (in addition to that in section 1(2) and schedule 1) about the ballot paper,

(c) specify documents and information to be forwarded to the Scottish Ministers by a counting officer under paragraph 10, and

(d) make provision for the creation of offences.

(3) An order under sub-paragraph (1) may not be made unless a draft of the statutory instrument containing the order has been laid before, and approved by resolution of, the Scottish Parliament.